Picture the Past

LIFE ALONG THE
NILE
RIVER

JANE SHUTER

Heinemann
LIBRARY

© 2005 Heinemann Library
a division of Reed Elsevier Inc.
Chicago, Illinois

Customer Service 888–454–2279

Visit our website at www.heinemannlibrary.com

Produced for Heinemann Library by
   Bender Richardson White.
Photo research by Cathy Stastny and
   Maria Joannou
Designed by Ben White and
   Ron Kamen
Printed in China

09 08 07 06 05
10 9 8 7 6 5 4 3 2 1

Library of Congress Cataloging-in-Publication Data

Shuter, Jane.
  Life along the River Nile / Jane Shuter.
    p. cm. -- (Picture the past)
  Includes bibliographical references and index.
  ISBN 1-4034-5827-8 (hardcover) -- ISBN 1-4034-5835-9 (pbk.)
  1. Egypt--Social life and customs--To 332 B.C.--Juvenile literature. 2. Nile River Valley--Social life and customs--Juvenile literature. I. Title. II. Series.
  DT61.S6446 2004
  932--dc22
                                         2004002361

Acknowledgements:
The publishers would like to thank the following for permission to reproduce photographs: Ancient Art and Architecture/John P. Stevens p. **13**; Ancient Art and Architecture/R. Sheridan pp. **9**, **11**, **19**; Heinemann Library pp. **10**, **14**; Peter Evans p. **30**; Phil Cooke/Magnet Harlequin p. **6**; Photo Archive p. **23**; Trustees of the British Museum, London pp. **16**, **20**, **26**, **28** (numbers 821-PS337236, EA2560-PS239457, EA9901/5-PS290776, EA4157-PS330979); Werner Forman Archive/Dr E. Strouhal pp. **12**, **21**, **25**; Werner Forman Archive/British Museum, London pp. **8**, **18**, **27** (numbers PH2638a, PH2843, PH1044); Werner Forman Archive/Shimmel Collection, New York p. **24**.

Cover photograph of a painting in the tomb of Ipy depicting fishermen casting their net reproduced with permission of Werner Forman Archive.

Every effort has been made to contact copyright holders of any material reproduced in this book. Any omissions will be rectified in subsequent printings if notice is given to the publisher.

Some words are shown in bold, **like this**. You can find out what they mean by looking in the glossary.

ABOUT THIS BOOK

This book is about daily life in towns and villages along the Nile River in ancient Egyptian times. The ancient Egyptian civilization lasted from about 3100 B.C.E to 30 B.C.E. The Nile runs the whole length of Egypt, and the country grew up around it. Most of Egypt is desert. There is very little rain. People depended on the river for food, drinking water, water to wash and cook with, and transport. Almost everyone lived and farmed along the river. Sailing along the Nile was the only way people could get from one end of the country to the other.

We have illustrated this book with photographs of objects from ancient Egyptian times and artists' ideas of town life then. These drawings are based on information that has been found by **archaeologists**.

The author

Jane Shuter is a professional writer and editor of non-fiction books for children. She graduated from Lancaster University in 1976 with a BA honours degree and then earned a teaching qualification. She taught from 1976 to 1983, changing to editing and writing when her son was born. She lives in Oxford with her husband and son.

Contents

The Nile River

The ancient Egyptians lived and farmed along the Nile River, using the soil to grow food for themselves and their animals. In ancient times, the Nile flooded each year from July to October. When the water went down, it left behind lots of mud that was a rich soil good for **crops.** The Egyptians used the river for water and for food—eating the fish that lived in it. The Nile was also the quickest and easiest way to travel around. The **pharaoh** used the Nile to send **officials** or soldiers to all parts of his kingdom.

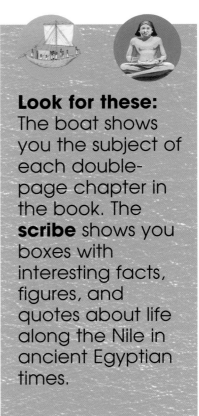

Look for these: The boat shows you the subject of each double-page chapter in the book. The **scribe** shows you boxes with interesting facts, figures, and quotes about life along the Nile in ancient Egyptian times.

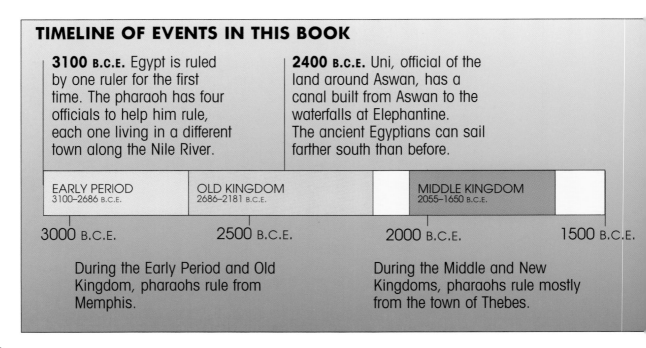

TIMELINE OF EVENTS IN THIS BOOK

3100 B.C.E. Egypt is ruled by one ruler for the first time. The pharaoh has four officials to help him rule, each one living in a different town along the Nile River.

2400 B.C.E. Uni, official of the land around Aswan, has a canal built from Aswan to the waterfalls at Elephantine. The ancient Egyptians can sail farther south than before.

| EARLY PERIOD 3100–2686 B.C.E. | OLD KINGDOM 2686–2181 B.C.E. | | MIDDLE KINGDOM 2055–1650 B.C.E. | |

3000 B.C.E.   2500 B.C.E.   2000 B.C.E.   1500 B.C.E.

During the Early Period and Old Kingdom, pharaohs rule from Memphis.

During the Middle and New Kingdoms, pharaohs rule mostly from the town of Thebes.

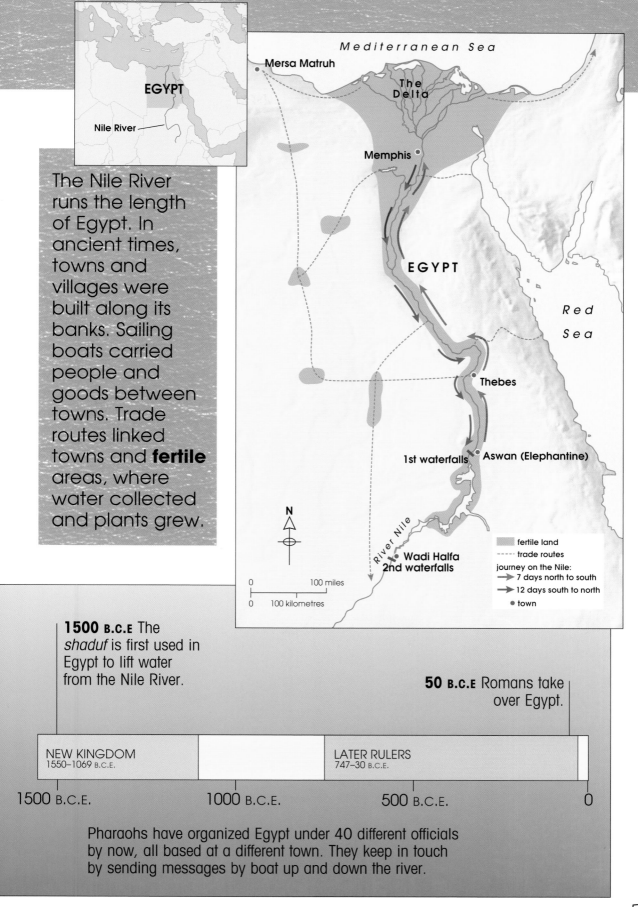

The Nile River runs the length of Egypt. In ancient times, towns and villages were built along its banks. Sailing boats carried people and goods between towns. Trade routes linked towns and **fertile** areas, where water collected and plants grew.

EGYPT

Nile River

Mediterranean Sea

The Delta

Memphis

EGYPT

Red Sea

Thebes

1st waterfalls

Aswan (Elephantine)

Mersa Matruh

River Nile

Wadi Halfa
2nd waterfalls

N

0   100 miles
0   100 kilometres

fertile land
trade routes
journey on the Nile:
7 days north to south
12 days south to north
town

1500 B.C.E The *shaduf* is first used in Egypt to lift water from the Nile River.

50 B.C.E Romans take over Egypt.

NEW KINGDOM 1550–1069 B.C.E.		LATER RULERS 747–30 B.C.E.	

1500 B.C.E.   1000 B.C.E.   500 B.C.E.   0

Pharaohs have organized Egypt under 40 different officials by now, all based at a different town. They keep in touch by sending messages by boat up and down the river.

Beside the River

The ancient Egyptians could grow **crops** only in the mud left behind when the Nile flooded. So they had fields all along the Nile River. Towns and villages were scattered along the edges of the fields, just above flood level. Most villagers were farmers. Farmers lived in towns, too, along with craftworkers, **traders,** and other workers and their families.

HAPY, RIVER GOD

An ancient Egyptian song to Hapy, god of the Nile River, says how important the river is, "He is father of the barley and the wheat. If he is slow to rise, people hold their breath then grow fierce as food runs out. When he rises well, the people and the land rejoice [give thanks]."

As in ancient times, many Egyptian farmers use a *shaduf,* a pole with a bucket at one end and a weight on the other, to lift water from the Nile River.

The mud that the Nile left behind needed lots of watering. The ancient Egyptians tried to trap as much floodwater as possible, so they did not have to constantly get water from the river. Each year they fixed the mud-brick **reservoirs** that they built to trap and hold floodwater. They also had a network of **irrigation canals** that filled with water during the floods and were refilled from the reservoir.

This picture shows how the water moved around the fields in canals.
Canals had:
- wooden boards that stopped the water, or let in when they were lifted
- paths around the edges
- bridges so farmers could move around easily.

The Seasons

There were three seasons along the Nile River. The **inundation** was when the river flooded. This lasted from July to October. Then came the planting season, from November to April. May and June were harvest months and were very busy. The fully grown **crops** had to be cut down and removed before the Nile flooded again, so the farmers had to watch the river closely.

Many ancient Egyptians used the Nile as a natural resource all year long. This man is hunting wild birds in the marshes along the riverbanks. He is using a small boat made from **papyrus reeds.**

During the inundation, farmers could not work in the fields. They spent some time fixing their tools and taking care of their animals. They also had to do **duty work** for the **pharaoh.** This was a set number of days of work that most people had to do. Some people paid others to do the work for them. Most farmers could not afford to do this.

DUTY WORK

There were different kinds of duty work, but most were difficult tasks. Just before the inundation, people had to clear out the **irrigation canals.** During the inundation, jobs included moving stone and doing basic building work on a **temple** or a pharaoh's tomb.

Scribes worked for the pharaoh all the time, so they did not have to do duty work. They kept records of everything, including the amount of **grain** collected during the harvest season on each piece of land, as shown here.

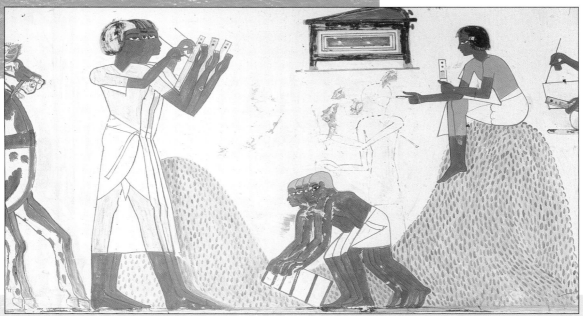

Farming

The people of ancient Egypt grew everything they needed to eat. The most important **crop** was **grain,** mostly barley and wheat. The ancient Egyptians used grain to make bread, **porridge,** and beer. Grain was the first crop the farmers grew after the **inundation.** Once this was harvested, they grew vegetables—mainly onions, leeks, cabbages, beans, cucumbers, and lettuce.

The ancient Egyptians used simple wooden farming tools. Tools used for cutting things, like the sickle in this picture, had cutting teeth made from sharpened stone or copper.

Farmers planted fruit trees and vines along paths, to give shade as well as fruit. Dates, figs, pomegranates, and grapes all grew well in the heat. Farmers kept bees, too. Honey was an important food because the ancient Egyptians did not have sugar. They used honey and dates to sweeten drinks and food.

ANIMALS

Cattle pulled the ploughs, and sheep and goats stomped the seeds into the soil and ate the stalks of grain after the harvest. These animals also were used for milk, cheese, and meat. Ducks and geese were kept for eggs and meat, while bees were kept for honey.

Farmers sometimes ploughed the soil using small wooden hand ploughs. Bigger ploughs were pulled by oxen, as shown in this ancient Egyptian tomb model.

Fishing

Most ancient Egyptians did not eat much other meat, but they ate a lot of fish. The Nile River was full of all kinds of fish, such as catfish and eels. They used small, lightweight fishing boats. The boats were made out of bundles of **papyrus reeds** tied together with rope. The fishers had to be very careful moving around in the boats, because they tipped over easily.

The ancient Egyptians often had paintings of fishing on the walls of their tombs. Because these paintings show the perfect world of the **afterlife,** their nets are always full of huge fish! This painting shows a large wooden fishing boat.

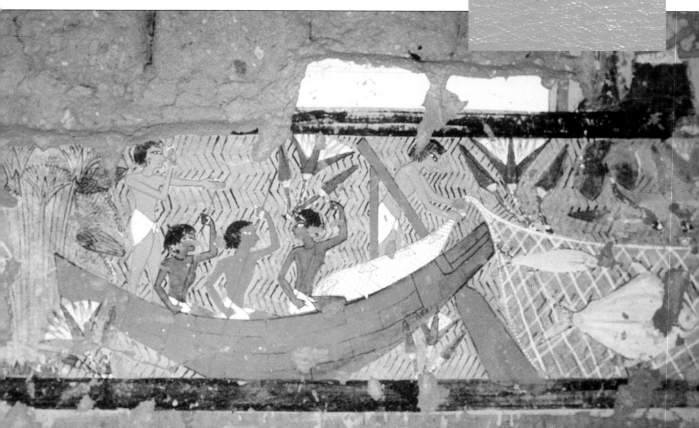

We know that some ancient Egyptians fished with poles that had bone or bronze hooks on the end of the fishing line. They caught only one fish at a time this way. A better way to fish was to take out two boats, with a net hung between them. Fish got caught in the net. All the fishers had to share the catch, but there was plenty to go around.

BEWARE OF CROCS!

The Nile was full of crocodiles as well as fish. Fishers must have been in constant fear of crocodiles. A **scribe** wrote, "Even if they get a good catch of fish, they still call out, blinded by fear, 'the crocodile's waiting!'"

When boats fished in pairs, one fisher paddled at the front and another at the back of each boat, while the others worked the nets.

Boat-Building

Ancient Egyptian **papyrus reed** boats did not have high sides, so they were more like rafts. The sailors used paddles to move the boats along. From about 3100 B.C.E., the ancient Egyptians began to use sails on the boats, so they could catch the wind and use it to move faster. They still used papyrus reed boats for fishing.

TOOLS

The ancient Egyptians built papyrus boats using nothing but their hands. They built wooden boats using simple axes and saws with copper blades.

The ancient Egyptians could sail a wooden boat from Memphis to Elephantine in about seven days, with their sails up, using the wind. This was a trip of about 430 miles (700 kilometers). The journey back, against the wind, took about twelve days.

The boat-builders made wooden boats from acacia trees, which grew well in the hot, dry weather. They used planks of wood that overlapped each other, tied together with rope. After about 2700 B.C.E., the ancient Egyptians traded with other countries for cedar wood, which gave much larger planks.

Wooden boats like this one were better than papyrus boats because:
• they were stronger
• the planks could be built up to make sides
• they were more waterproof
• they lasted longer
• they were better for long journeys
• there was more space for the sailors.

Trade

The first people to live in ancient Egypt traded from village to village, swapping food, clothes, pots, and baskets with each other. They did not travel far to trade, or trade with other countries. In about 3100 B.C.E., Egypt began to be ruled by one ruler, the **pharaoh.** Other countries saw it become a powerful, organized country. They began to want to trade with Egypt.

Things brought in from other countries were mostly expensive, such as perfume, wood, silver, jewels, and even certain animals like giraffes. This silver cup came from Greece.

The ancient Egyptians used the Nile to carry trade goods as much as they could. Traders sometimes used small **papyrus reed** boats to move goods short distances. They used wooden boats with sails for longer distances, or for goods that took up a lot of space. When they had to carry goods across the desert, they used donkeys. The goods were packed in baskets hung over the animal's back. In ancient times, there were very few camels in Egypt to use for transport.

If the Nile did not flood much one year, there was less soil for growing **crops.** So people had less **grain** at harvest time, and the pharaoh had to trade for grain from other countries. **Scribes** measured how much grain was put in and taken out of grain stores, as shown in this picture.

17

Houses and Homes

Ancient Egyptian houses were made from mud bricks. Wealthy people lived in the biggest houses. They had bathrooms where they poured river water over themselves to wash. The water drained away through a hole in the floor. For toilets, they used buckets with wooden seats, which they washed out with water and then emptied in the fields. Most people just used the fields as toilets and washed in the river.

Some houses, like this one, were built on a mud-brick platform instead of directly on the ground. This was probably in case the water level of the Nile rose too high during **inundation.**

Most ancient Egyptians did not have much furniture, or other belongings. Most people had wooden beds, but poorer people slept on a mud-brick platform instead. They had stools for sitting on, and one or more small, low tables. Folding stools and tables could be carried to and from the roof more easily.

GARDENS

Because Egypt was so hot and dry, gardens were not common. Water for them had to be brought from the river. Wealthy people had gardens with ponds, which they filled with fish and ducks. They grew trees that gave shade and food, like date palms and pomegranate trees.

Among the objects buried with ancient Egyptians were models of their houses. This model shows the doorway, window, and courtyard of a house.

Clothes and Makeup

The ancient Egyptians wore as little as possible, because of the heat. Fishers just wore a short piece of cloth wrapped around the waist. Women wore a **tunic.** Young children often wore nothing at all. Ancient Egyptians had dark skin that was not likely to burn, but people did get very hot. This is one reason why they kept their hair short, or even shaved it off.

People wore wigs made from human hair or, if they could not afford this, plants. One ancient Egyptian wig, like this one, was found with the head lice still in it from the person whose hair was used to make it!

LAUNDRY

Most people had their washing done for them, as homes did not have running water. Washing was done in the Nile River. Only men did the laundry. Crocodile attack was always a danger around the river.

Both men and women wore makeup made from plants or minerals. They wore kohl eyeliner for practical reasons, as well as to look good. A thick black line around the eye reflected sunlight and kept it out of the eyes, similar to sunglasses. Kohl had a chemical in it that drove away insects that lived along the riverbanks. It also helped prevent eye infections. Grown-ups often wore perfume, too. They mixed it into fat, and put it on their wigs. When the fat melted, it gave off a nice scent.

Most ancient Egyptians wore white clothes because white reflects sunlight and stays cooler. Wealthy people, like this **official** and his wife, wore several layers of very thin cloth that was more expensive because it took longer to make.

Estates

In ancient Egypt, all the land belonged to the **pharaoh.** He kept some land for himself. He divided up the rest into large areas called estates. Each estate was run by an **official.** The officials had to give the pharaoh a share of all their animals, **crops,** and the goods their workers produced. Most people did not own land. They worked a piece of land on an estate.

On this small estate there was:
- a big house for the family that ran the estate
- a garden for the family
- store rooms
- workshops
- homes for the servants
- stables for the horses (not pictured)
- a wall around all of this
- farmland between the estate and the Nile.

store rooms

garden

farmland

family house

workshops

wall

servants' homes

Once a year, all the animals on an estate were brought together and counted. This tomb model shows a cattle count. People were rewarded or punished depending on the health of their animals and how many young ones they had produced.

Scribes on the estate kept records of everything—how much seed was planted, how much **grain** was grown, how many animals there were. The pharaoh could ask for this information at any time. Estates had their own stores for grain from the harvest each year, and gave it out to the workers each week. Some of the grain was saved to use as seed the next year.

ALL YOU NEED

Estates were not just big houses with farmland attached. Most of them had their own workshops that made everything that anyone on the estate needed. They had workers who made cooking pots, shoes, and cloth.

Religion

These amulets, or charms, show Sobek, the crocodile god. Ancient Egyptians wore amulets to keep them safe from danger, but these have no holes for a string to tie them on. They were probably buried with a dead person, so they could have Sobek's protection in the **afterlife.**

The ancient Egyptians believed in many gods and goddesses. Some gods, like Amun, were worshipped all over Egypt. Others were worshipped in just one place, or by some people more than others. Fishers worshipped Sobek, the crocodile god, hoping he would keep them safe from the crocodiles in the Nile. Hapy was the god of the Nile. They wrote songs for him.

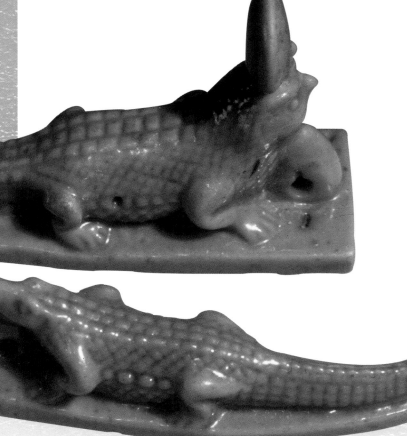

Temples were built as homes for statues of the gods and goddesses, and places to leave them offerings. They were not buildings for ordinary people to worship in. Most people often only went to temples for yearly **religious festivals,** when the statues were taken out for everyone to see. At other times, the people worshipped at **shrines** set up along the riverbank, or in their own homes. Shrines were often just a small mud-brick altar, with a shelf to hold the offerings.

Priests prepared the dead for the afterlife. This painting shows priests praying in front of a mummy in his case before it was put in its tomb.

25

Funerals

The Nile River was an important part of the **funeral ceremony.** The ancient Egyptians believed that the dead came back to life. So they preserved their bodies and buried them with many belongings. They did the preserving, called embalming, in open-sided tents down by the river. The river provided water to wash the bodies and for the purification (cleaning) ritual during embalming. The breeze from the river carried away the smell of the chemicals used in embalming.

Water was important in many of the stages of burial, to purify the body. In this painting, one priest, in a jackal mask, holds up the mummy case while another priest sprinkles water on it.

Cemeteries were often on the opposite side of the Nile River from the towns and villages where people lived. People did not like living too close to the dead, but they wanted to visit the cemeteries often, to pray to their lost relatives and friends and to bring them gifts. The ancient Egyptians did not build bridges across the Nile, so there was always a ferry that ran between the cemeteries and the places on the other bank.

Family members took the body of a dead relative by ferry boat across the Nile to the cemetery, as shown in this ancient Egyptian tomb model.

Food

The ancient Egyptians did all their cooking outside. They cooked bread in special ovens. They cooked almost everything else in pots over an open fire, either on the mud-brick roof or in a courtyard. People ate outside, too. They ate their main meal in the cool of the evening. At breakfast and lunch they mostly ate bread with vegetables or cheese.

This tomb model shows servants brewing, baking, and butchering meat in the kitchen of an estate. These jobs were not actually done in the same place at the same time.

Egyptian recipe—flat bread

This bread has to stand to rise for about two hours between mixing and baking. You can leave it alone for this time. WARNING: Ask an adult to help you with the cooking.

1 Dissolve the yeast in 2 tablespoons of the warm water. Add a pinch of sugar. Leave until frothy (10 minutes).

2 Mix the salt and flour in a bowl.

3 Pour the yeast mix into the flour. Mix with your hands. Add more warm water, slowly, until you have a squishy dough. Push and fold the dough (add flour if it gets sticky) until smooth and a bit stretchy.

4 Put a little oil on your hands. Roll the dough in it, replace in the bowl and cover with a cloth. Leave in a warm place for 2 hours. The dough will grow to twice its size.

5 Push and fold the dough again. It will lose air and get smaller. Break it into pieces the size of a small orange.

6 Turn the oven on as high as it will go.

7 Flatten the dough pieces on a floured board until about 1/3 inch thick. Put on an oiled tray, cover, and leave for 20 minutes. Once the breads rise, cook them in the oven for about 8 minutes.

The Nile Today

Egyptian people still live along the banks of the Nile River. In some ways, their lives are the same as their ancestors'. For example, some farmers still use a *shaduf* to lift water from the **irrigation canals.** There is one way in which life is very different. In 1902 a dam was built at Aswan, to control the flooding of the Nile. Since then, the flow of the Nile has been regulated, so the land has enough water for **crops** to grow throughout the year.

Modern Egyptians use many different kinds of boats on the Nile River. *Feluccas,* like this one, are similar in design to the small wooden boats used by the ancient Egyptians.

Glossary

afterlife perfect place ancient Egyptians believed they went after death

archaeologist person who uncovers old buildings and burial sites to find out about the past

cemetery place where dead people are buried

crop plant grown to provide food or to sell

duty work set number of days each year that people had to work for the pharaoh. Scribes did not have to do this work, but everyone else did.

fertile rich, good for growing things

funeral ceremony ritual that is done when a dead person is buried

grain seeds of some grasses that can be eaten. Barley, wheat, rice, oats, and rye are all grains.

inundation time when the Nile River flooded its banks

irrigation canal ditch dug to carry water from one place to another

official person who helps run a country

papyrus reed Egyptian plant used to make paper and other things

pharaoh ruler of ancient Egypt

porridge soft food made by cooking grains in liquid

religious ceremony/festival special time when people go to one place to pray to the god and goddesses

reservoir specially dug pond where water is stored

scribe person in ancient Egypt who could read or write. Scribes helped officials and pharoahs run the country.

shrine place where people come to pray to gods and goddesses and leave them gifts

temple large building where many people pray together to gods and goddesses and leave them offerings

tunic T shirt-shaped clothing, knee-length or longer, worn mostly by women in ancient Egypt

More Books to Read

Shuter, Jane. *Ancient Egypt: Builders and Craftsmen.* Chicago: Heinemann Library, 1999.

Shuter, Jane. *Ancient Egypt: Farming and Food.* Chicago: Heinemann Library, 1998.

Thames, Richard. *Ancient Egyptian Children.* Chicago: Heinemann Library, 2002.

Williams, Brenda. *Ancient Egyptian Homes.* Chicago: Heinemann Library, 2002)

Index